Get Productive in a Multi-task World

A PARENT'S GUIDE TO PROJECT MANAGEMENT

JULIA DONNELLY AND LINDA SANDERS

authorHOUSE®

AuthorHouse™
1663 Liberty Drive
Bloomington, IN 47403
www.authorhouse.com
Phone: 1-800-839-8640

First published by AuthorHouse   10/14/2011

ISBN: 978-1-4634-2547-0 (e)
ISBN: 978-1-4634-2548-7 (sc)

Library of Congress Control Number: 2011911243

Printed in the United States of America

Table of Contents

Introduction—What Will I Get Out Of This?

This guide will explain project management and provide you with practical advice on how to apply it. Most corporations and government agencies recognize that projects must be managed to be successful. During the later part of the twentieth century, a lot of effort went into developing a common way of establishing and controlling a project, resulting in a set of standards that can reduce work effort and position an organization to complete projects on time, as planned, and on budget. This same approach can be easily used for your projects at home, at school, in your religious or social organization, and even in your day-to-day activities. This guide was created for you.

A "project" is simply an effort that has a beginning and an end, with a series of activities in between and has an outcome. Think about how many projects you have managed in your life including group outings and social events. These projects required you to manage the effort to achieve positive results. As you read this guide, you will recognize some of the steps. You may even find them to be simply "common sense". Project Management is just that. However, without a disciplined approach steps can be easily overlooked when you are faced with the challenge of managing any project.

Collectively, we have been project managers for over forty years. We have successfully implemented many projects. As we meet people, we find most have tried to manage a project of some sort. The key difference between us and the others that have attempted to manage projects is that we are both trained and experienced in the "art" and "science" of project management.

According to the Project Management Institute's A Guide to the Project Management Body of Knowledge (*PMBOK*), project management is about employing a series of principles that enable you to plan, initiate, control, and close a project. In short, you will find project management is about enabling you, the project manager, to keep costs low, save time, reduce stress, and retain harmony while delivering successfully. The principles and methodology described in this guide have worked for large corporations for years. These same practices can be applied to your projects regardless of their size or your available money or time.

We have successfully delivered many projects using the techniques that we have outlined in this guide. We are confident that you will have the same success.

You have successfully completed many projects. So, why do you need this guide?

We will help you recognize what made your projects successful so that you can repeat those efforts that worked and avoid the pitfalls.

Julia Donnelly and Linda Sanders

In a Hurry?

We understand that reading this short guide might not fit into your busy schedule. Here is a quick reference.

Step 1: Define your Project – Initiate Phase - This is not an option!

a. Be sure that you understand what is expected to be delivered; this includes what is included in the project, as well as what is expected to be left out. Understand what is optional and what is necessary to be successful. This may be helpful if you need to prioritize activities.

b. Understand how much money you have and how much money you expect to spend.

c. Identify any constraints. This includes any limitations that are placed on you, your team, your time line and your final product.

d. Recognize any assumptions that are being made.

e. Document what you believe that you are expected to deliver or anticipate achieving at the end. Review it with others to ensure that you have a common understanding.

Step 2: Determine the actions (Phases and tasks) that you need to do to complete your project – Plan Phase

a. Write down or create an electronic list of the tasks and the relationships of multiple tasks. Be sure that you understand any dependencies of tasks to each other and the task sequence that is needed to complete your project.

b. Determine the people, your team; individuals that you need to complete the project (skills, availability).

c. Assign tasks to people.

d. Develop the project schedule.

Step 3: Identify risks, obstacles that you need to consider which could have a negative effect on your project, your team or on your final effort – Plan Phase

a. If the number of risks you identify is high or the severity of risks is high, be sure to Stop, Think and Assess the overall value of your time and the effort of the project.

b. Review and analyze risks throughout the life of your project.

Step 4: Create and manage your budget – Plan Phase

a. Prepare a budget so you can monitor and control your expenses.

b. Do not allow unplanned work or purchases without identifying the impact to your budget. You may need more money.

c. If you must take on more work and make unplanned purchases and there is no additional money available, scope back the work or purchases that have already been planned from your project. Stay on budget.

Step 5: Manage changes that could distract or derail your efforts – Execute Phase

a. It is nearly impossible to identify all your project requirements, money, time, people, etc., at the beginning of your project.

b. Your effort should always be directed to minimize change.

c. Create a process with your team on how changes will be requested and communicated, how they will be analyzed and how a decision to proceed will take place.

d. Project scope creep is one of the most common reasons for project failure.

Step 6: Control your efforts – Control Phase

a. To keep control over the project you will need to:

    1. Use your project plan as a check list to make sure everything gets done.

    2. Have regularly scheduled team meetings. Here you will get team member updates, hear about problems, and identify how far along you are.

b. Respond to problems, don't ignore them. Common problems are due to people related issues, unforeseen predicaments, requirements they you didn't consider at the beginning or an underestimated timeline.

c. Your actions and your attitude are important to the overall success of the project.

d. Decide up front with your team how and when you will communicate.

Step 7: Celebrate your success – Close Phase

a. Reward the team.

b. Recognize the individual and team contributions.

c. Acknowledge the effort; be grateful.

Chapter 1: Welcome to Project Management

Your son comes home from school and informs you that you were "volunteered" to coordinate the upcoming school fund-raiser in three months. Do you have a project? What do you do next?

What Is a Project?

A project is a temporary venture taken to create a product or service. It has a clearly defined start and end; there are actions that need to be taken and people available to "help," definitive goals, and boundaries. Sound familiar?

Now that you know what a project is and recognize that you have a project, let's get started with understanding project management.

What Is Project Management?

The widely accepted definition of project management (PM) is the application of knowledge, skills, tools, and techniques to a broad range of activities to achieve an end. Project management practices are best described in terms of the processes and knowledge areas that are associated with them. It is a sequential series of tasks that need to be identified and performed in order.

The processes can be placed into five phases: Initiating, Planning, Executing, Controlling, and Closing. In addition, there are nine knowledge areas: project integration management, project scope management, project time management, project cost management, project quality management, project human resource management, project communications management, project risk management, and project procurement management.

That's a lot to know. Can you make it easier for me?

Project management is easily translated into our definition, which is the use of common practices, skills, and controls that can be used consistently and orderly to achieve an objective. This is done through a series of activities that start and end at certain points in time and produce meaningful results.

Successful project management requires the use of both hard and soft skills. Hard skills are things that you learn and apply. They include reading, writing, and math. They also include things like building a web site or cooking. Soft skills are the interpersonal skills that you acquire by watching and listening, or from experience. They include managing people and having positive work ethics, a good attitude, and a desire to learn. Once mastered, these are the skills that make a difference in your ability to lead, negotiate, and get along with others. As important as it is to apply the hard skills that you will learn about as you read this handbook, it is critical that you gain appreciation for the people, or soft skills that are essential to a successful project, including leadership, team building, and problem solving skills.

The key to a successful project is to follow the best practices of project management regardless of the size of the project. Obviously, all projects are different. However, the fundamental steps that must be taken are the same. And while you should scale the work to the project, be sure to follow the all of the steps outlined in this guide to ensure that your dollars and time (and the time of your team) are used wisely and that you will achieve your objective.

In short, what is Project Management?

Project Management is about knowing what you are trying to achieve, planning, and then delivering on the expectations.

Why Should I Know about Project Management and Learn the Methodology?

Project Management works. It eliminates problems. It is a discipline used in just about all businesses. The practice continues to grow in government agencies, in the military, and in the corporate world. Entrepreneurs, for-profit and not-for-profit agencies that deliver a service or product commonly use this methodology. Organizations around the world implement common project management processes, disciplines, and standards to deliver their projects on time, within budget, without surprises, and with the quality that they expect. They are using common Project Management processes to successfully introduce large projects and the same processes can help you.

Why Do Projects Fail?

There are some general reasons why projects fail. Failure occurs when you don't deliver what you were attempting to achieve, when the costs are too high, or when you don't complete the project on time. Does this sound familiar?

Common causes for projects to fail include the following:

- Leadership is lacking.

- There is no defined goal, or it is not commonly understood.

- The right people are not working on the project.

- Team members are not accountable.

- There is no planning.

- Timelines are not achievable.

- There is no delegation of activities.

- Projects risks are not addressed.

- There is a lack of clear communications.

- Changes are introduced without controls.

Planning and preparing for a project will make a difference! We will show you how.

What Makes Projects Successful?

Our experience has shown us that projects succeed and stress is managed when these actions are put into place;

- The project is defined. You understand what the expected results will be.

- There are clearly stated objectives.

- Commitments are agreed to and contracts are signed (if applicable).

- There are reliable estimates of time and money.

- Everyone on the team is aware of their roles and responsibilities.

- A detailed project plan has been developed and agreed to by all members of the project team.

- A single individual is responsible for monitoring the plan.

- A well-organized project notebook is maintained through the life of the project.

How do you measure success?

A project is considered successful when it is delivered on time and on budget. But the real testimonial to a successful project is the satisfaction of the person that requested it.

Are You Already a Successful Project Manager?

More likely than not, you have completed some very successful projects. You should be proud of those efforts. As you probably have experienced, they aren't easy. But is the process that you used repeatable? Do you have the time or stamina to do it again? Could you have done things better? The key to successful project management is the reliance on tools, templates, and practices that you can use again and again.

You need to manage the team.

Remember, people manage projects; projects don't manage people. Therefore, it is important to consider your role as the project manager. You are the leader, and your leadership style is critical to your ability to deliver. As the project manager, you need to control the scope of the project, monitor activities and expenses, and ensure that risks are mitigated. In addition and equally important, you need to motivate, provide direction, create belief, encourage independence, award positive behaviors, and make success feasible.

Have you ever noticed that the "right" people for your team never seem to exist? Even if they do, it is highly likely that they will not be available to help. Your ability to create excitement and energize your team members—whoever they might be—is critical. They are the right people. They are the only team members that you have.

Team members need to believe that they can do it. This requires that you define roles and responsibilities for every individual on your team that fits their skills and ideally, their interest and experience. Be sure to include those team members who are working directly with you, as well as those who are casually associated with the project. People like to be part of a winning team. Your job is to make them succeed by creating a winning environment. Winning attitudes and positive self-images among your team members make a difference. Go team!

The Winning Team

I can't do it alone. How do I pick the right people for my team?

Like an orchestra that produces a remarkable sound, a successful project team makes beautiful music too. The team is a blend of the talent, knowledge, and insight of its members, making the best of the unique potential of each to produce something meaningful. We have found that the most successful teams have the following characteristics:

- A project team must be able to draw on individual talents, as well as collective energy.

- A project team is agile. Members are able to take action with some uncertainty. They are accountable for their actions and encouraged to take risks.

- There must be a single objective for the team to achieve. Working with a sense of purpose creates energy among the team members. On the other hand, continuous pressure creates burnout and disillusionment. Motivation to perform creatively occurs when team members are interested, enjoy what they are doing, and are satisfied and challenged by the work.

- A team must be able to exercise creative thinking. The opportunity to share ideas without fear of being stifled or belittled is critical. Creativity is fostered in an environment where there is an aim for quantity rather than quality of ideas.

- A successful team values the contributions of the individuals.

- A strong team works collaboratively and experiences excitement. In these conditions, individuals contribute their unique skills to the effort. As a result, team members often gain knowledge from each other.

The Project Life Cycle

A project has five key phases according to *PMBOK*:

1. Initiating

2. Planning

3. Executing

4. Controlling

5. Closing

These five phases provide the framework for project management. No matter how small or large the project is, following all five steps is important. Of course, consideration should be given to the size of the project, the time available, and the number of people on your team. Some phases will take less time for smaller projects and more time for complex projects with larger budgets, more team members, and greater risks. However, these fundamental steps should be taken for every project.

You are now ready to get started. Read carefully, follow the instructions, and have fun!

Chapter 2: Project Initiation

Initiating a Project

Every project starts at the beginning. In this first phase, you need to determine your objective, identify what tasks will or will not be included, establish any assumptions, and recognize any risks. This is also the phase of the project where you identify your schedule and determine what you are delivering. This helps you to determine if your project is even feasible.

Let's revisit the school fund-raising project as an example. Before you begin planning the event, ensure that you have the interest and support from key participants in your effort. Does the school administration support the effort? Do you have support from the parents? Is there interest from the children? Is money available? Will you have the help that you need? What are the interests from those that you are trying to accommodate? Is there a goal?

Think about all of the people, and issues that you could encounter for your project before you get started. Listen carefully to those individuals you are trying to accommodate. Remember that a project is successful only if you meet the project objective.

Once you know that you have a reasonable project, start your project notebook.

Project Notebook

The project notebook is your collection of project artifacts, essential to your success. It will be your source for all important documents not only for this project, but a reference for future projects. As you proceed through this guide, we will instruct you on what needs to be included in your notebook, as well as those documents that are nice to have.

A loose-leaf binder works just fine. It makes accessing the documents that you need easy and organization convenient. Use a separator for each phase of the project for easy reference. Consider exercising some creativity by decorating the cover of your notebook. A little construction paper and markers can bring life to your binder. It will also help to distinguish multiple projects.

You may also consider an electronic document if you are not dependent on having paper. Consider creating a FACEBOOK page for your project, an Excel document, or any electronic document. A web page can also work.

Project Charter

The project charter is your first document in the notebook. The charter is your contract or formal agreement with the individual that requested the project, as well as the team. If there is no one else on the project, the charter is still relevant. It is your way of taking stock or inventory of what you are trying to accomplish.

Having an effective charter is a good way to communicate and gain consensus from others. It helps everyone understand what you expect to deliver and how you plan to realize your goal. Document what you know, believe, or anticipate.

What Do I Need to Write a Charter?

A charter communicates the limitations of what you can and cannot deliver and why the project is important. In the charter, you should include the following:

- Identify what you are going to deliver (when and how, if you know).

- Estimate how much money you expect the costs to be over the life of the project. (You will have opportunities to revisit this.)

- Determine what help you might need.

- Identify any assumptions and constraints (things that might present an obstacle).

- Identify who needs to approve the final product or service, as well as how you will know if you are successful.

School Fund-Raising Project Charter

Here is a sample charter for our school fund-raiser:

- **Objective:** The project objective is to raise money for the school to purchase new playground equipment. In addition to raising money, the effort is intended to be both fun and educational for the participating students. While encouraging personal growth, the fund-raising will enable the students to develop team-building skills and to have fun in a safe environment.

- **Scope (What is in and out):** The fund-raising will take place over three months and be limited to the students in grades four through six. The money will be used to purchase the equipment and fund any project-related costs. Building the playground is not included in the scope of this project. A separate project will be established to manage that activity.

- **Deliverables: This is what you are going to produce as an outcome of your project.**

  - Prizes (Individuals participating and those who raise the largest amount of money will be eligible for a reward.)

  - Goods and Services (the means by which funds will be collected)

  - Marketing (the means to create enthusiasm and encourage participation by the students, as well as the parents, school administration, and community)

- **Costs:** To cover the anticipated expenses, $1000 is available from the Parent/ Teacher Association. Any additional costs are expected to be covered by the proceeds of the project. Total costs are expected to be $2500. This total cost will be revisited with each Phase of the effort.

- **Constraints:**

  - The fund-raising event must not coincide with any other fund-raiser that is planned for a school activity.

  - Administration of the event must occur during normal school hours.

- **Assumptions:**

  - At least one-third of the total eligible student population will participate.

  - The $1000 committed by the PTA will be available at the onset of the project.

A project charter template is provided in the Appendix.

Once I Finish the Charter, What Do I Do with It?

Share it. The charter isn't intended to be kept in a drawer. Place your charter in your notebook. It is important. It demonstrates that you have this project under control. You understand and can communicate what you intend on delivering.

Just as important, you can tell others what you are doing so that you can reach agreement and get volunteers.

For our school fund-raiser project, consider sending the charter to the PTA members, the school administration, and even the students and their parents. An electronic copy will do. Use this opportunity to solicit the help of others.

Once you have your charter, you are ready to start planning.

Key Activities for Initiating a Project		
	Key Activities	Recommended Techniques
Project Manager	• Determine project objectives, scope, and purpose • Determine high-level deliverables and their estimates • Determine high-level constraints and assumptions • Determine what you need to complete the project (i.e., people, facilities, etc.) • Write the project charter	Prepare your notebook Write a project charter

Chapter 3: Planning

Planning a Project

This is the most important part of the project. Doing this up front makes a difference throughout the project. The effort spent planning can save countless hours of confusion and extra work in the subsequent phases of the project. There are nine steps in the planning process.

In the planning phase, you determine what you need to be successful, when you will get the work done, and who will do it. You also determine the order of the tasks. The most critical outcome of this effort is the project plan.

The plan gives you the means to monitor the work effort. It is also a good way to communicate to team members what you expect them to do and when.

Where Do I Start?

Step 1: Define your project deliverable(s)

A deliverable is the tangible result of the completion of a task or tasks. Simple deliverables may be signs for the event or the prizes (for the school fund-raiser). Start planning by identifying as many deliverables as you can think of for your project.

Step 2: Break deliverables down to components (work breakdown structure)

After you have listed your deliverables, identify the activities that need to be completed for each. Break the work down to tasks and subtasks, smaller segments of work effort. The outcome is called a *work breakdown structure* (WBS).

The WBS is simply a way to identify all of the work needed to make your project successful. Any activity that might have a cost or require someone to take action should be included, if known. By creating a WBS, you can easily organize your effort. The WBS can be presented in a graphic form or in an outline. An example of each is shown below for our school fund-raiser project.

School Fund-Raising Project Outline

Level 1- School Playground Fund-Raiser

Level 2- The Components (marketing, prizes, and events)

Level 3- Key categories of activity to attain each component (signs e-mails, all participant prizes, school picnic, etc.)

It makes sense, but do I create the WBS alone? I don't know everything that needs to get done.

Certainly, you shouldn't do this alone. The most effective means of creating a WBS is to involve your team. However, experience tells us that the WBS best starts with the Project Manager. If you have a similar project that you can refer to, use it. If not, start with things that you know make sense and create a draft. Your team will help you validate the tasks that you defined. A skeleton WBS gets people thinking about what needs to get done and what they may be able to offer. It is a great way to encourage those volunteers to get involved.

Step 3: Define Tasks

Once you have your WBS, further break down individual tasks. No task should take longer than twenty hours. Break longer tasks into multiple tasks. This will help you keep the plan manageable and team members accountable.

For example, in our fund-raiser project, suppose you envision fifty dozen cookies for a bake sale. Making the cookies will likely take more than twenty hours. Consider turning this activity into multiple tasks. This can be done by breaking the effort into baking cookies of a particular type (i.e., butter, chocolate chip, etc.). If multiple bakers are available, split the task among them. Assign each baker a specific number of cookies or a particular type.

Managing a project with tasks that take less time enables you, the project manager, to track progress easily and react quickly if a delay is experienced or an individual is not able to deliver on time.

Step 4: Identify resources and make assignments

Now go through your plan and identify who will do the work and when the work should be completed. Do this for all of the identified tasks.

Be sure to consider everyone on your team and all of the tasks that have to be completed. Consider family members, friends, specialists, and consultants. Don't forget to assign yourself some tasks too. Allow time for pulling the team together for progress reporting, meetings, and celebrations of milestones.

When you are making assignments, consider if you need a particular sequence of events. For example, you can't get signage until you have determined when the events will occur. Tasks that must occur before others are called *predecessors*. A late predecessor could have an effect on every task that is associated with it.

Make task ordering easy. Assign a number to every task. Then, associate tasks to the assigned number. Consider using Microsoft Project software, an Excel spreadsheet, or a simple sheet of paper.

Step 5: Project schedule development

This step takes most of your time, but is most important to your success. At this point, you need to secure your schedule for the project. You must determine how long each task that you identified in the earlier step should take and when each should start and end.

Once you have identified all of the tasks that are needed, develop a schedule. When scheduling, consider that although a particular task may only take three hours, you may not have that time available to you without interruption. Three hours may have to be spread across multiple days, and you must consider the total amount of time required. This is referred to as *elapsed time or duration*.

There is a difference between *effort* and *duration*. Suppose you plan to start a task on Friday, but you only have two hours in the morning, and on Saturday you are at ball games all day. In addition, you have invited the family over for Sunday dinner, and you have to work on Monday. The next time that you will work on your task is on Tuesday. The task effort is three hours, but the project schedule shows the task starting on Friday and ending on Tuesday. The total task duration is five days. As you can see, a simple three-hour effort may have duration of five days. Track the total duration to ensure that you have adequate time.

Now you are ready to put in dates for your tasks. Work with a calendar and your team and put your schedule together.

Poor scheduling can result in a project failure. Do not underestimate your time or the time of team members. You will experience a loss of control if you have unrealistic deadlines.

By establishing your plan, you are defining your *critical path*. This is the optimum sequence and duration to complete the project and an indication of which efforts are critical to timely completion of the project. Tasks on the critical path that fail to complete on time put the overall project at risk. Keep your eye on these tasks, as they are particularly important to your success.

Step 6: Anticipate Risk

All projects have risks. During this planning phase, take time to identify potential risks. Performing a risk assessment adds value to managing your project, and planning contingencies allows you to take action when a problem arises. Risk, by definition, is the probability that an event or events will occur and will have a negative effect. A project is considered successful when it is completed on time, and on budget. Performing a risk assessment may eliminate the surprises that can cause failure.

Risks can change your project's scope, quality, schedule, and budget. Risk is high in the early stages of the project, which is why performing the assessment early in the project is important. This won't be the only time that you conduct this assessment, unless your project is small or the risks are minimal. Otherwise, this exercise should be conducted throughout the life of the project. As your project develops, some risks go away, but new risks can be presented.

Here are steps to perform a risk assessment, identifying the potential risks within your project, their impact, and the probability that they will occur. This enables you to plan for the risk, to take actions to reduce the likelihood of occurrence, and (for the most significant risks) to develop a contingency plan.

Risk Identification Process

You must identify risks that could affect your project.

Work with others to identify risks. Even if you are working alone on a project, bring friends together to help identify potential risks to your project. This allows you to draw upon more experience and get different perspectives.

This is a good exercise for your team members. It gives them the opportunity to share concerns. Here is your opportunity to demonstrate your leadership skills.

Here are some risks you may put on your list:

- You do not have experience with this type of project.

- Team members have never worked together before.

- The money may not be delivered in time.

- There are multiple, conflicting fund-raisers scheduled for the same time.

How Do I Conduct a Risk Assessment Session?

Step 1: Hold a meeting.

Invite individuals with an interest in or something to contribute to the project. Encourage the team to be open and candid. Keep points clear and directed. This is the participants' opportunity to share any thoughts or suggestions about what may go wrong with the project.

Follow the tips for conducting a meeting in Chapter 6.

Step 2: Identify what could go wrong.

Start with your suggestions. But, getting everyone involved is important.

Ask the team for advice. Give everyone Post-It notes or 3" by 5" cards. Ask everyone to write down things that could threaten the project. Identify all legitimate and manageable risks. Place one risk on each note.

Step 3: Determine impact and probability.

After collecting thoughts and suggestions from team members, take the following actions:

- Collect the notes or cards from each participant.

- Group the risks into categories (examples: external factors, quality, and people). Eliminate redundancies.

- Review the risks with the participants. Is the list complete? Have you considered everything that could affect your success? Reach consensus on the final list.

- Determine the severity of risk impact on the project and the probability of a risk occurring. Each event must be evaluated individually. Your assessment should look something like this:

Item	Risk Description	Impact	Probability	Overall Risk Level
	What could happen?	*What is the significance of the event?* *High (3), Medium (2), or Low (1)?*	*What is the likelihood that the event will occur?* *High (3), Medium (2), or Low (1)?*	*Multiply the **impact** by the **probability** to determine the **overall risk level**. The higher the level, the greater attention the risk requires.*
1	There is no experience with the company providing goods; they may not deliver on time.	3	2	6
2	The money from the PTA may not come in time to produce the marketing materials.	2	1	2
3	None of the activities yield enough money to pay the expenses.	3	3	9

Use the words "legitimate" and "manageable" to filter from consideration any risk that is not a true threat to project success or any issue over which the project team has no control. For example, in our school fund-raising project, we have no control if enough money isn't raised for the playground, but we can plan backup activities, just in case. We may not be able to avoid the risk, but we can establish a contingency plan.

Review the outcome of your risk assessment. Do you see a lot of ratings of 9? If there are a significant number of highly rated risks, Stop! Think. Assess the overall value of your time and effort for this project. Should the project stop? Are the risks too high to continue to spend your time and the effort of your team? Stopping a project because the risks are high is not a negative reflection of the project manager. In fact, it is the sign of a project manager that has control of the project

How do I deal with the risks, after they have been identified?

There are four tactics for dealing with risks as presented in the Project Management Institute, *A Guide to the Project Management Body of Knowledge*:

1. **Avoid** the risk and its potential consequences. This can be done by changing the project management plan and eliminate the risk completely. An example of avoiding a risk is to reduce the project scope.

2. **Mitigate** the risk by changing one of the four key project dimensions: scope, budget, schedule, or quality. Any predictable risk can be managed with this tactic.

3. **Transfer** the impact. While this is not a common approach, identify who or where can the risk be transferred. Consider your options (i.e., purchase an insurance policy or seek professional consultation).

4. **Accept** the risk and its potential consequences. This generally works if the overall risk is low.

Risk is organic. The probabilities and impact to a project change over time. Review and analyze risks throughout the life of your project. A risk assessment should not be a onetime event.

Step 7: Create a budget.

In this step, you prepare a cost estimate. This budget is used to monitor and control expenditures during the project. A variety of methods may be used to estimate cost, depending on the level of detail available to you. Some costs gathered for the school fund-raiser project include the costs of the marketing material, prizes, and the equipment.

Estimating the budget should be done at each phase of the project. Be sure to revisit the money that you expect to spend as you refine your resources, deliverables, and expectations.

How do I adjust if I start to exceed my budget?

What you actually spend and planned expenses should always be tracked. If you find through your monitoring that you are spending over budget, use these proactive techniques to get back on budget as quickly as possible:

1. Implement "zero tolerance" scope change. Ensure that no unplanned work or purchases are added to your project. Any additional effort or expenses must get preapproval. This doesn't mean you won't take on the additional work or purchase. It means that must find room in the budget for all proposed work before moving forward. You may have to go back to the project initiators and ask for more money.

2. If you are lucky enough to have a contingency budget, this may be the time to use it. Money set aside for contingency is separate from the project budget and should be used if you are likely to exceed the budget due to estimating errors.

   As the school fund-raiser project manager, consider maintaining 50 percent of the PTA allocation at the onset of the project. If you don't need the money for the effort, consider returning it or using it for a celebratory event for the team.

3. Scale back the work. If all else fails and you're not able to get additional money, you may need to remove some of the work or purchases from the project. There may be options to complete this project on budget with less than what was planned. Here is your opportunity to exercise creativity.

Step 8: Practice control of project changes

When working on a project, you will likely not get all of your requirements up front. Did you forget to ask your party guests if anyone is vegetarian? Did you anticipate that a member of your team would have to leave town early? Managing those things that are not expected is done by establishing a *change management practice* early in your project.

Change is defined as an activity that occurs within the life of a project that could impact one of three things: (1) scope—what you are delivering, (2) time—when you will be ready to deliver, or (3) quality—the completeness and accuracy of what you will deliver. Change can occur, and in fact, you should consider this a natural part of the project and highly likely.

Every effort should be made to minimize changes. Follow these simple steps when someone on your team comes to you with a "brilliant" idea or wants to modify a task:

1. Communicate. Encourage team members to keep you informed when a change occurs. As the project manager, it is your role to be notified and to direct the necessary actions.

2. Give it some thought, and then think some more. Before the team examines the impact, the initiator should consider the importance of the request. (Is it essential? Can I substantiate this request?)

3. Ask for the request in writing. Be sure that the initiator documents the rationale. If it isn't important enough to write about, it is likely not important enough to pursue.

4. Analyze the request. This is the opportunity for you to lead team members (or select team members) in an analysis exercise. Consider the impact of the request to the overall project. What value does this change bring to the overall project? Is the absence of this change significant? Will it be noticed? Does it reduce the overall value?

   Other questions to ask include: Will addressing the change increase the amount of time needed to deliver? Will our resources still be available? What does or does not occur if we are late? Is a cost associated with the increase in time? If so, are the funds available? Can the change be considered for delivery in the future, after the initial project is complete?

5. Communicate. Once you decide to proceed with or to forego the change, inform your team. Let your members know the impact your decision has on their responsibilities and due dates. Give them the opportunity to react with questions or concerns. Once you have the team's approval, update the project plan, and you are ready to proceed.

6. Repeat. Replicate this process each time a team member suggests a "brilliant" idea after your scope, schedule, and budget have been secured.

Be very aware of what is known as "scope creep." Increasing scope increases work and increases the timeline of your project. If not controlled, scope creep will cause your project to slowly go out of control. The scope of a project doesn't change by itself; team members or others associated with the project are contributing. Recall, the scope is identified in the first phase of a project. The scope states the objectives of the project and the necessary work. It describes what is included and what is excluded from a project. As a project evolves, expectations sometimes change or requirements are missed at the onset. This results in change that can significantly impact timelines, the budget, or quality. Therefore, you must manage change to ensure that you can deliver successfully. A change control process helps you manage those inevitable changes.

How do I manage change?

It is almost impossible not to have some scope creep. You should strive toward effectively managing scope creep instead of preventing it. Here are some ideas for managing scope creep:

- Have a project plan.

- Define and prioritize tasks, requirements and deliverables.

- Define risks.

- Ask questions.

- Don't take scope creep personally—avoid getting defensive.

- Have a scope change process.

- Enable multiple opportunities for the team to exchange discoveries and changes.

Scope creep is one of the most common reasons for project failure, causing projects to go over timelines and over budget. The best way to minimize scope creep is to define the requirements up front as thoroughly as possible. To minimize scope creep, set achievable goals, prioritize requirements into must-haves versus nice-to-haves, and define the risk for each must-have requirement

Step 9: Develop a Communication Plan.

A communication plan needs to be developed for your project so your team will know how they give and receive information and the expected time of the communication. Here are some examples of communications for your plan:

- weekly team meetings (no more than 1 hr.)

- weekly status updates from team members regarding accomplishments, problems, issues and affect on timeline if any. Status reports can be e-mailed if it is not convenient to meet in person.

- status update to the Project Sponsor at agreed upon time frames.

See Appendix B for an example of a Communication Plan Template.

Step 10: Hold a kick-off meeting.

Hold a project kick-off meeting to get your team together and create enthusiasm. You should communicate your goals and expectations, team members' responsibilities, the project schedule, and your deliverables. This is also the time for the team to identify gaps in these areas and resolve them.

See Chapter 6 for information on "Conducting Effective Meetings" for more suggestions.

Planning Key Activities		
	Key Activities	**Recommended Techniques**
Project Manager	• Define your project deliverable(s) • Break deliverables down to components (work breakdown structure) • Define tasks • Identify resources and make assignments • Develop project schedule • Identify critical path • Anticipate risk • Create a budget • Create a change control process • Hold your kick-off meeting	• Prepare an organization chart and a contact list • Prepare roles and responsibilities • Develop a work breakdown structure (WBS) • Estimate effort and duration of tasks listed in your WBS • Develop a communication plan • Identify risks and assess impact to your project • Determine quality standards, if applicable • Determine change control procedure • Obtain project team approval of project schedule • Hold kick-off meeting, if applicable, and identify gaps in key activities

Chapter 4: Execution and Control

You have planned your project, organized your team, determined everyone's roles and responsibilities, identified risks and mitigation plans, established a budget, developed a communication plan, and officially kicked off your project. Now it's time to get going. Your time and attention will be focused on keeping the momentum, making sure that the tasks are completed on time, and monitoring the project budget. Of course, you need to ensure that all of this is done with quality in mind. This is done by maintaining control.

How do I deliver success?

To keep control over a project, you can use the artifacts that you created earlier on in the project:

- Project Plan: Here is your opportunity to use the detailed plan that you created. This plan serves as a checklist to ensure that the tasks you identified are completed.

- Team Meetings: These meetings give you opportunities to hear firsthand about the health of the project. A combination of individual and team meetings ensures that you are getting accurate information and can address problems promptly. Consider lunch meetings or fifteen-minute phone calls to accommodate complex schedules.

- Team meetings are important chances to get updates, hear about issues, and share successes. Encourage team members to provide timely, precise, and honest updates.

- Deliverables: By examining the status of all deliverables and the time estimations against the progress that has been reported by your team, you can determine the feasibility of meeting your target.

Essential to managing and controlling projects is free, open, and honest communications between members of your team and yourself. Communicate, communicate, and communicate!

How do I handle issues that might come up?

If everything is going well, you're lucky, and you will have to do very little. Most of the time, your attention will be focused on responding to problems. Common problems are due to people-related issues, obstacles presented by unforeseen predicaments, requirements that you didn't consider at the onset of the project, or underestimated timelines. There is no right or wrong way to address these problems. However, your actions and your attitude are important to the overall success of the project. Consider these factors in your responses:

- Know when to take action. There's an old adage: "A project slips one day at a time." Early detection of problems is critical, and that is why you have regular team meetings and discussions.

- Decide whether to address the problem now or in the future. This may be an ideal time to demonstrate patience.

- Avoid micromanaging, a challenge gotcha for some project managers. Avoid the temptation to supervise every action and decision. You don't want team members to think you don't trust them.

Execution and Control Key Activities		
	Key Activities	**Recommended Techniques**
Project Manager	• Review all created artifacts for the project: for example, the charter with list of deliverables, project plan, and communication plan • Run team meeting or individual sessions to check on progress • Indentify risk/ prioritize / determine impact • Determine how to deal with each risk event and how will you mitigate the risk • Make contingency plans for risks • Respond to problems	• Conduct a brainstorming session to identify risks • Determine which tactic you will use for each risk • Use template in Appendix B • Hold team meetings and share outcomes • Use a change control procedure • Follow the communication plan • Manage the project plan

How do I handle risks to my project's success?

We talked about risk in Chapter 3, but risk assessment and review are ongoing processes that take place throughout the life of your project. Follow the steps listed in Chapter 3.

Learn from your problems.

Learn from the issues that you encounter during your project. Stop. Ask yourself and your team members the following:

- Could this problem happen again? If so, how can we prevent it?

- If we can't prevent the problem, how can we mitigate it?

- Does this problem affect other aspects of the project?

Taking the time to reflect on problems will help you and others on your team learn from experience.

Change: it is inevitable.

Chapter 5: Team Building

Team Building: What Is It and Why Do It?

According to Wikipedia, an online community-built encyclopedia, *team building* generally refers to "the selection, development, and collective motivation of result-oriented teams. Team building is pursued via a variety of practices, such a group self-assessment and group-dynamic games and generally sits within the theory and practice of organizational development."

The process of team building includes:

- Clarifying the goal, and building ownership across the team

- Identifying the inhibitors to teamwork, removing or overcoming them. If they cannot be removed, mitigating their negative effect on the team.

To assess itself, a team seeks feedback to find out both:

- Its current strengths as a team

- Its current weakness as a team

To improve its current performance, a team uses feedback from the team assessment in order to:

- Identify any gap between the desired state and the actual state

- Establish an approach to address, anticipate or remove gaps going forward

Feedback and Measuring Effectiveness

Team members need feedback throughout the project. Team members should also be encouraged to give you and the other team members' constructive feedback. It is an important part of project management. It provides the means to improve performance, address issues, and recognize positive performance.

Follow these important rules when delivering feedback:

- Feedback has to be timely, meaning it must be given when the issue occurs.

- Give feedback regularly.

- Don't tell people what they want to hear—be honest.

- Let everyone be heard.

- Don't let it get personal.

By evaluating feedback, you can adapt the communication plan to ensure that you are meeting the needs of the audience at any given point in time. This enables continuous improvement.

Now, what does this mean to you? Why do you care about team building? To be honest, you don't always have to care about team building. If your team only involves you and a couple of people who know each other, then you can just get to work and complete your tasks. Your job is to develop an overall sense of teamwork.

On the other hand, if you have a group of people who don't know each other, you may want to do some team building so people feel comfortable working together. It is important to make sure everyone understands the expected outcomes and why they are participating. Your job as project manager is to get the team involved, committed, organized, and working effectively. How do you do this?

Successful team building creates effective and focused work teams. As the project manager, you need to pay attention to these elements:

- Communicate your expectation for the team's performance and expected outcomes. Make sure all members understand why the team was created.

- Do your team members want to be on the team? Are the team members excited and committed?

- Are team members working together effectively?

- Are team members clear about the priority of their work/tasks?

- Do the members feel responsible and accountable for the team's achievements?

- Are all team members involved in the decision-making process?

Team-Building Icebreakers

Icebreakers are great to use at meetings to get people comfortable and to instill trust. You can find lots of free ideas for team icebreakers by conducting an Internet search on "team building icebreakers." Just make them fun, and get everyone involved; no criticism from anyone is allowed.

A popular icebreaker often called "speed dating" may not improve your love life but can be a quick, nonthreatening approach to getting to know members on your team. It works like musical chairs. Follow these easy steps:

1. Create a series of questions that have to be asked. The questions should not be threatening but should give the interviewer an opportunity to express his or her interests, describe his or her job, or introduce you to his or her family.

2. The team is split in half.

3. Seating is arranged so that chairs are paired, one facing another.

4. One half of the team stays seated along one set of arranged chairs. The other half of the team will rotate.

5. Following seven minutes of conversation, a bell is rung, and the team members on the rotation team move to the next chair.

6. Once all of the rotating team members have met the seated members, the teams change position. And the rotation begins again.

7. By the time that both teams have completed the rotation, everyone has met everyone.

Chapter 6: Conducting Effective Meetings

Meetings are great tools for generating ideas and managing group activities. Always remember that this face-to-face contact can fail without adequate preparation and leadership.

Preparing for Meetings

Start your meeting right by setting a time that allows all participants to prepare and to travel from their jobs and homes. Announcing the time and day of the week for getting together should be something you, the project manager, should do at the very beginning of the project. Always prepare an agenda, and supply any notes you may have from a prior meeting. Ask your team to review the material before the meeting. This increases the probability that the team will be prepared.

The success of the meeting depends a great deal on the skills you display as the meeting leader. Here are the minimum things you should do to ensure a successful meeting:

- Issue an agenda.

- Start the discussion and encourage active participation.

- Do your best to keep the meeting pace comfortable—try not to move through the agenda too quickly or too slowly.

- Summarize what was discussed and give any recommendations at the end of each agenda item or logical section.

- Make sure all participants receive the minutes of the meeting promptly.

- Consider serving food, maybe a little dessert. You might be surprised to see the friendship that develops.

Managing a Meeting

Choosing the right participants is key to the success of any meeting. Make sure the people with the necessary information for the items on your agenda are invited. As the leader of the meeting, work hard to ensure that everyone's thoughts and ideas are heard and that there is a free flow of debate. No single individual should dominate the discussion.

At the end of the meeting when all agenda items are resolved or action is agreed upon, make clear who in the meeting is responsible for each action item and its timeline. Add to your minutes the action item, the person responsible for the action item, and the expected completion date.

Time Keeping

Meetings are notorious for eating up people's time. With so little extra time on your hands, managing your time and the time of others effectively is critical. Here are some ideas to keep your meeting brief:

- Start on time.

- If someone comes to the meeting late, don't recap what has been said. This sends the message that it is OK to be late.

- At the beginning of your project, lay down the ground rules for meetings. If you fail to do so at the start, it may be too late to change bad habits midway through the project. Make everyone accountable for their actions.

- State a finish time for the meeting, and don't let speakers run over—that means you too!

- Arrange your agenda so that the most important topics are discussed first in case you can't finish all the agenda items in the time frame arranged for the meeting.

- If you finish the agenda items before the stated end time, stop the meeting and let everyone go. Most people appreciate getting a few minutes back in their day.

Issuing Minutes

Minutes of your meeting are important. They record decisions of and actions agreed to by the team. Minutes also provide a record of the meeting and provide a document to review and use at your next meeting. Keep them brief. Focus on decisions and actions that require follow-up.

Chapter 7: Influencing People

As a project manager, you will frequently find yourself in situations where you need to influence people. Listed below are ways to influence others, as well as ideas for when to use a particular style.

Persuading

- Proposing: Ideas, suggestions, recommendations

- Reasoning: Facts and reasons to support your position or counter another's

Persuading is useful when the issue is open to rational discussion and when you are not in a highly competitive or emotional situation.

Asserting

- Stating expectations: Demands, needs, requirements

- Evaluating: Positive or negative judgments of the other person

Asserting is useful when you have legitimate needs or expectations and stand to lose something if they are not met. You are in a position to offer incentives and/or exert pressure to gain agreement.

Bridging

- Involving and supporting: Soliciting different views, encouraging

- Listening: Paraphrasing or summarizing, reflecting back feelings, asking for clarification

- Disclosing: Letting uncertainty show, admitting mistakes, asking for help

Bridging is useful when you need the other's commitment, value his or her input, and are open to influence. It is also useful when the other person is angry or upset.

Attracting

- Visioning: Articulating an exciting possibility or ideal outcome

- Finding common ground: Highlighting areas of agreement; appealing to common values, interests, hopes

Attracting is useful when you want to generate excitement, a sense of purpose, or team spirit. This method is also effective when you and the others share important values and hopes and when team members trust your motives.

Moving Away

- Disengaging: Reducing tension or changing conditions while continuing to pursue objectives

- Avoiding: Giving in or withdrawing to avoid personal discomfort

The moving away technique is useful when existing conditions inhibit productive work, and a postponement or change in conditions will help you achieve your objectives.

Chapter 8: Closing

Your project was a success. Congratulations. Make time to take stock of what you have learned. Keep in mind that project management is as much a science as an art. You learn from your experiences and from the experiences of others. Therefore, find as many opportunities as possible to be involved in projects. You learn what does or doesn't work from other project managers. You also grow from your experiences as a project manager.

Celebrate a job well done. Reward the team. Recognize the individual and team contributions. It is important to acknowledge the effort.

Conduct a Lessons-Learned Exercise

Shortly after a project has finished is the ideal time to reflect back on what worked and what could have been done better. Don't wait. This should be a team effort that is performed while the experience is still fresh. The outcome can be instrumental in ensuring that future projects reflect those things you learned from this project.

There are critical steps to a lessons-learned exercise. First, ask someone who wasn't on the team to facilitate. This enables you and the other team members to contribute. Don't forget that you are a member of the team and have thoughts, suggestions, and comments that should be considered if you have the opportunity to conduct a meeting.

When conducting the exercise, follow these guidelines:

1. Tell participants that this is not intended to be a personal attack. Participants should be encouraged to state facts and offer constructive criticism.

2. The facilitator should encourage everyone to participate. Brainstorming works well for these sessions, even in small groups. Use two sheets of paper tacked to the wall: one marked "What Worked" and the other "What Didn't Work." Ask participants to shout out items for each category. The facilitator should mark every comment on the paper. Sample items to be considered are:

    a. Project leadership

    b. Team member participation

    c. The scope of the effort

    d. The amount of time allotted

    e.   The amount of money allotted

3.   After all of the comments have been recorded, the team should look for trends. This can be done in a collective exercise or by the facilitator after the brainstorming session is complete.

In a follow-up session, reconvene the team to consider the items collected during brainstorming. Revisit each of the items to determine what did and did not work. For what worked, determine what contributed to the successful outcome to ensure similar success in future projects. For what didn't work, determine why and what can be done to avoid each pitfall next time.

The results should be written and shared with every team member.

File the meeting outcome in your project notebook. Refer to it the next time that you think that you have a project. It will be instrumental in your success.

Closing Meeting

A final meeting with the team to review the outcome of the lessons-learned exercise and secure any follow-up issues enables everyone to bring closure to the effort. Take a deep, collective sigh.

Celebrate

At the introduction of this guide, we told you that the key to your success would likely be the people on your team and your ability to manage them. People appreciate being recognized. Recognizing them at the end of a project makes them more likely to contribute on your next effort.

The celebration doesn't have to be elaborate. A simple thank-you note would do. Be sincere. Identify the individual contributions of the team member. Cite specific tasks that this individual completed. Consider challenges that the team member faced. Think about the hours that the individual contributed or the skill or talent that made a difference.

A team celebration is always appreciated. Following the stress that often happens in a project, having a party is a nice way to relax and reflect on the team's efforts. As the project manager, it is still critical that you recognize the individual contributions. While the recognition should always be sincere, consider fun ways to demonstrate your appreciation.

For the school fund raiser project, consideration for a team roast will offer a humorous way to look at the individual contributions. Awards for the most innovative solution, the individual who was always on time, or the team member who best demonstrated the spirit of collaboration will give the team a chance to have a laugh, recognize contributions and consequently, will likely keep team members open to volunteering in the future.

Thank You

Well we hope this handbook has helped you to understand the processes and mechanisms of project management and how to pull a project and your project team together.

We also hope that you enjoy the challenge of leading projects and enjoy the satisfaction that comes from a successful result. We know leading and managing is a challenge, but it is possible to get productive in a multi-task world. Thank you for letting us share our thoughts with you.

To get downloadable templetes referenced in the book, ask questions or share feedback, please visit our website at http://beproductivebooks.com/.

Appendix A: Checklists

Project Management Checklist

The following is a quick reference to the project phases, the tasks and the materials that need to be developed and, or maintained during a particular phase of the project. Remember that you won't be using all of the phases or all of the materials for every project. The size and scope, as well as the risks associated with the project will determine the amount of rigor you want to apply. When in doubt, rely on the reference materials to guide you.

Initiation Phase	
Actions	Kick-off meeting
Artifacts	Identify who and how many people you need on your team.
	Estimate a budget.
	Secure high-level requirements.
	Create the project charter.
	Create the project notebook.
Planning Phase	
Actions	Refine the requirements.
	Identify the team members.
	Conduct a risk assessment.
	Define team behaviors.
	Introduce team review meetings.

Artifacts	Risk assessment
	Roles and responsibilities
	Communication plan
	Project schedule
	Work breakdown structure
	Defined work effort
	Critical path
	Project milestones
	Assignments
	Change control process
	Budget
Executing Phase	
Actions	Manage project progress.
	Hold progress meetings.
	Manage changes and concerns that arise.
Artifacts	Project schedule.
	Documentation of your status.
	Issue log.
Controlling Phase	
Actions	Conduct review sessions.
	Conduct quality reviews.
	Track progress.
	Conduct risk reviews.
	Manage changes.

Artifacts	Risk assessments Change control forms
Closing Phase	
Actions	Finalize and update all documents. Conduct and document lessons learned Conduct and document closing meeting
Artifacts	Collect final versions of project documentation.

Appendix B: Project Notebook

The notebook is your single reference for all of your significant project artifacts. It should contain the following for each phase of your project:

1. Initiating
    a. Contact list
    b. Project charter
    c. Roles and Responsibilities

2. Planning
    a. Work breakdown structure
    b. Project budget
    c. Project plan
    d. Risk Assessment Worksheet
    e. Communication plan
    f. Meeting notes

3. Executing and Control
    a. Change control process and requests
    b. Meeting notes
    c. Problem Solving Worksheet
    d. Status Report

4. Closing
    a. Lessons learned

Project Notebook

Sample: Contact List

Be sure to get contact information for each team member at the onset of the project. Once received, ask if the information can be shared with the other team members. By sharing the names and contact information among the team members, you are encouraging them to interact and help each other. This is particularly important if issues need immediate attention. It is also a good way to get your team to personalize the project.

Name:	
Address:	
Preferred method	Cell phone: Home phone: Work phone:
Preferred contact time:	
E-mail address:	

Project Notebook

Sample: Project Charter

[Insert Project Name]
Project Description
Explain why this project exists, the goal, and why it is important and to whom.
Approach
How do you intend on carrying out the project?
Scope - In
What is included in the project?
Scope - Out
What is not included in the project?
Goals / Measures of Success
Identify how you will know that you achieved success.
Stakeholders
Who are the principles in this project? They may include individuals that you are dependent on for money or time.
Product Deliverables
Describe what service or good you will provide as a result of this project.
Assumptions
Identify any ideas or notions that you expect to have in place to successfully implement your effort.
Risks
List all risks identified, their probability, and their impact on the project
Constraints
List all project constraints (example: deadline date of all deliverables)
Approval(s) (if needed)

_____ _____

Name   **Signature**   **Date**

Project Notebook

Sample: Meeting Notes

<Project Name>	
Meeting date:	
Facilitator:	
Attendees:	
Decisions:	
Action items: (description, responsible person, due date)	
Date and time of next meeting:	

Project Notebook

Sample: Project Plan

Use all or some of the items presented in the sample. Consider the number of people that you have on your team, the amount of time that you have to get the work done and the risks that you may have in your project to determine how much detail that you need in your plan.

Task No.	Task	Effort (days)	Scheduled Start Date	Scheduled Completion Date	Actual Start Date	Actual Completion Date	Predecessor	Resources
	Initiation							
	Develop Project Charter							
	Identify project stakeholder							
	Finalize scope (what is in and out of scope)							
	Determine goals & deliverables							

Task No.	Task	Effort (days)	Scheduled Start Date	Scheduled Completion Date	Actual Start Date	Actual Completion Date	Predecessor	Resources
	Determine constraints/ assumptions							
	Identify project team							
	Approve/notify team members							
	Establish/communicate team member expectations/roles							
	Develop charter							
	Review charter with stakeholder							
	Update charter as required							

Task No.	Task	Effort (days)	Scheduled Start Date	Scheduled Completion Date	Actual Start Date	Actual Completion Date	Predecessor	Resources
	Obtain stakeholder approval							
	Communication Plan							
	Develop communication plan (mode and frequency)							
	Review plan with stakeholder and team							
	Obtain stakeholder approval							
	Develop Project Plan/ Schedule/Calendar							
	Develop project plan/ schedule/calendar							

Task No.	Task	Effort (days)	Scheduled Start Date	Scheduled Completion Date	Actual Start Date	Actual Completion Date	Predecessor	Resources
	Define project deliverables(s)							
	Break deliverables down to components							
	Define tasks and identify resources to assignments							
	Determine effort							
	Determine schedule							
	Identify critical plan							
	Identify risk							

Task No.	Task	Effort (days)	Scheduled Start Date	Scheduled Completion Date	Actual Start Date	Actual Completion Date	Predecessor	Resources
	Review project plan/schedule/calendar with team							
	Update project plan/schedule/calendars required							
	Obtain project team approval							
	Obtain stakeholder approval							
	Budget							
	Create budget							
	Change Control							

Task No.	Task	Effort (days)	Scheduled Start Date	Scheduled Completion Date	Actual Start Date	Actual Completion Date	Predecessor	Resources
	Create change control process							
	Kick-Off Meeting							
	Review charter							
	Review communication plan							
	Review project plan/schedule/calendar							
	Update documents requiring change							
	Distribute to team for final review							

Task No.	Task	Effort (days)	Scheduled Start Date	Scheduled Completion Date	Actual Start Date	Actual Completion Date	Predecessor	Resources
	Publish documents							
	Requirements							
	#1 Req Mtg							
	#2 Req Mtg (high level picture)							
	#3 Req Mtg (drill down on requirements)							
	Conduct review session							
	Resolve any outstanding issues for acceptance							

Task No.	Task	Effort (days)	Scheduled Start Date	Scheduled Completion Date	Actual Start Date	Actual Completion Date	Predecessor	Resources
	Obtain requirements acceptance							
	Project Execution and Control							
	(Team tasks are listed here along with reviews and approvals.)							
	Project Closure							
	Survey(s)							
	Documentation completed							
	Project closure							

Task No.	Task	Effort (days)	Scheduled Start Date	Scheduled Completion Date	Actual Start Date	Actual Completion Date	Predecessor	Resources
	ONGOING ACTIVITIES							
	Status reporting							
	Issue/change resolution							
	Revise project charter, as necessary							
	Update project plan							

Project Notebook

Sample: Change Control Request

XXXXX – Project Name	
Priority: Determine how important is this change to meeting your project objective.	
Requestor:	**Date:**
Description of requested change to the project: ***Identify any Attachments:***	
Impact Analysis Result: (cost and time)	
Authorized by: (if required) **Name:** **Signature:**	**Assigned To and Date**
Action Taken:	**Change Completed Date**

Project Notebook

Sample: Communication Plan

The following table is used to outline the communication events that will occur to support your project.

Communication Events					
Event	**Communicator**	**Audience**	**Channel**	**Timing**	**Feedback Mechanism**
Example: Status Reports	*Project Manager*	*Project Team and PTA*	*Written reports* *Status review*	*Weekly on (day)*	*Face-to-face or e-mail*

Project Notebook

Sample: Status Report

Regularly inform your team of the progress being made. This is particularly important after you achieve a major milestone and for lengthy projects. It keeps the team motivated. Interest in a project often dwindles after the initial days, weeks, or months.

Consider posting updates on FACEBOOK or send Twitter messages. The key is that you are keeping your team members informed and engaged.

The product of the meeting or the report should include the following:

1. Attendees (if meeting conducted)

2. Date and time of meeting

3. Status summary
   a. Accomplishments achieved
   b. Project plan deviations
   c. Schedule
   d. Effort/resources
   e. Key project/policy decisions
   f. What is scheduled between now and the next meeting

4. Significant project problems and issues

5. Risk and mitigation plan

Project Notebook

Sample: Problem-Solving Worksheet

Project Name:

Date:

Problem #:

Impact on Project:

Alternatives:

Recommendations:

Project Notebook

Sample: Risk Assessment Worksheet

Item	Risk Description	Impact	Probability	Overall Risk Level
1	*What could happen?*	*What is the significance of the event?* *High (3), Medium (2), or Low (1)?*	*What is the likelihood that the event will occur? High (3), Medium (2), or Low (1)?*	*Multiply the impact by the probability to determine the overall risk level. The higher the level, the greater attention the risk requires.*

Project Notebook

Sample: Issue Log

Tracking No.	Define	Impact	Responsibility	Anticipated date for resolution	Resolution	Date Resolved
01	The sign maker is unable to find and secure the permits to hang posters in the neighborhood.	Minimizes the marketing presence and could result in less-than-ideal participation	Sue	November 6	Sue aided the sign maker by engaging the local commissioner.	November 4

References

Baker, Sunny and Kim. *The Complete Idiot's guide to Project Management.* Alpha books, 2000.

Project Management Institute. *A Guide to the Project Management Body of Knowledge (PMBOK Guide)- Fourth Edition.* Project Management Institute, Inc. 2008.

Cleland, David I. *Field Guide to Project Management.* John Wiley & Sons, Inc. 1998.

Heerkens, Gary R. *Project Management.* New York: McGraw-Hill, 2002.